STE
FRENCH
Cooking

KÖNEMANN

BASIC FRENCH PANTRY

Most of the ingredients for French cooking are familiar to everyone and available everywhere. Anything that cannot be purchased at your local supermarket or delicatessen can usually be made at home or replaced with a suitable substitute.

Allspice: A berry which has the flavor of cloves, nutmeg, and cinnamon. Used as a flavoring in sweet and savory foods.

Bouquet Garni: Bunch of herbs used for flavoring dishes such as casseroles and sauces. Consists of parsley, thyme, bay leaf, and peppercorns tied in a cheesecloth bag.

Chicken Pâté: Smooth chicken liver paste available from delicatessens and supermarkets.

Caramelize: To cook sugar slowly until it turns the color of caramel.

Cracked Wheat: Whole wheat grains which have been cracked or broken during the early stages of milling the flour. Used for its nutty texture. Also called bulgur.

Croustade: Fried bread or pastry case used to hold fillings.

Dill: Herb used to flavor soups, sauces, salads, and pickles.

Eggplant: Egg-shaped vegetable with smooth shiny purple skin and creamy white flesh. Also known as aubergine.

French Mustard: Condiment prepared from mustard seed, herbs, oil, and vinegar. Used to flavor savory dishes. French mustard is spicy but not "hot". The most famous French mustard comes from the town of Dijon and is clearly labeled "Dijon mustard". It is milder than most mustards and perfect with delicate meats such as veal and chicken.

Gruyère cheese: Hard cheese with a minimum fat content of 27 per cent. It is related to Emmenthal. Swiss Gruyère is sweeter than the French variety.

Gougére: Choux pastry made from water, fat, and flour which forms a base for other ingredients.

Herbs: Unless otherwise specified, use fresh herbs in these recipes. The predominant herbs in French cooking are those that make up a bouquet garni — parsley, thyme, and bay leaves — as well as tarragon, dill, and basil. If fresh herbs

are not available, use one-third the quantity of dried herbs. For instance, 1 tablespoon chopped fresh herb or 1 teaspoon dried herb, crushed.

Hull: To remove the stem from the tops of strawberries.

Horseradish: Root of the horseradish plant. Commercially made horseradish is a mixture of grated horseradish root, oil, vinegar, and sugar.

Lard: Commercial pig fat available from refrigerator sections of supermarkets. Sold in blocks the same way as butter.

Leeks: A mild-flavored vegetable from the onion family. Select small to medium-sized leeks for best flavor. Substitute with green onions, if necessary.

Melba Toast: Thin slices of crustless bread, dried in the oven till crisp. Also available in supermarkets.

Olive Oil: Oil from ripe olives. Used in most Mediterranean styles of cooking.

Parmesan Cheese: Hard cheese used to flavor foods. Available in block form, shredded, or grated. Keeps longer in block form. Strong in flavor.

Watercress: Green leafy plant of the mustard family. It has deep rounded green leaves and a peppery taste. Use in sandwiches, salads, soups, or as a garnish.

Red Wine Vinegar: Refined vinegar made from red wine.

Tarragon: A flavorful herb, often used in chicken dishes. It is also used to flavor vinegar and is an important ingredient in Béarnaise sauce. French tarragon, when crushed between your fingers, will release a sweet pungent scent.

Vinaigrette: An oil-and-vinegar salad dressing. It can be made in a food processor in large amounts and stored in the refrigerator for several weeks. It is made from olive oil, wine vinegar, Dijon mustard, and pepper. Olive oil hardens when it is refrigerated, so allow to stand at room temperature about 30 minutes before adding to salad.

Add onions to the skillet and cook till well browned, about 20 minutes.

Add the garlic and sugar. Cook and stir till the sugar dissolves.

Add vinegar, flour, broth, water, wine, and sherry. Cook and stir till thickened.

Brush oil over both sides of bread and sprinkle with grated Parmesan cheese.

SOUPS & SUPPERS

*These can be served as a first course or, with a salad,
as a lunch or supper entrée.*

French Onion Soup

Preparation time:
15 minutes
Cooking time:
45 minutes
Serves 4–6

1/4 cup butter or
  margarine
1 tablespoon olive oil
4 large onions, thinly
  sliced
1 clove garlic, crushed
1 tablespoon sugar
2 tablespoons red
  wine vinegar
1/3 cup all-purpose
  flour
14 1/2-ounce can beef
  broth

1 1/4 cups water
1 cup dry white
  wine
1/2 cup dry sherry
2 tablespoons olive oil
1 clove garlic, crushed
1 small loaf French
  bread, cut into 3/4
  inch thick slices
1/2 cup grated
  Parmesan cheese
Parsley

---

1 In a large skillet heat butter or margarine and 1 tablespoon oil. Add onions and cook about 20 minutes or till tender and brown.
2 Add garlic and sugar; cook and stir till sugar dissolves and turns brown. Add vinegar and cook for 2 minutes more.

Sprinkle flour over onions. Cook and stir for 1 minute. Stir in beef broth, water wine, and sherry. Cook and stir till thickened and bubbly. Reduce heat and simmer, uncovered, for 25 minutes.
3 Preheat oven to 400°. In bowl stir together 2 tablespoons

oil and garlic. Brush over both sides of bread. Sprinkle one side of the bread with Parmesan cheese. Place bread on a baking sheet. Bake 5 minutes or till bread is crisp and golden.
4 To serve, place a slice of bread in the bottom of each soup bowl. Ladle soup over bread and garnish with parsley.

HINT
It is important that the onions are well browned to give the soup an authentic flavor. The sugar helps to caramelize the onions. Start with high heat for the first part of the cooking, then reduce to medium heat to brown the onions slowly.

Prawn Croustade

Preparation time:
45 minutes
Cooking time:
25 minutes
Serves 6

1/2 loaf unsliced bread *1/2 cup olive oil* *1 clove garlic, crushed* **FILLING** *1 pound prawns or* *large shrimp* *1 1/2 cups water* *2 slices lemon* *3 tablespoons butter* *or margarine* *6 green onions, chopped*	*3 tablespoons all-* *purpose flour* *Freshly ground pepper* *1/3 cup whipping cream* *1 tablespoon lemon* *juice* *1 teaspoon dried* *dillweed* *Dill sprigs (optional)* *Lemon peel (optional)* *Lime slices (optional)*

1 Preheat oven to 400°. Remove crust from bread and cut into 2-inch thick slices. Cut each slice diagonally to form a triangle. Cut a ¼-inch border around the bread slices and scoop out the centers, leaving some on the bottom.

2 Place bread shells on a baking sheet. In saucepan heat oil and garlic. Brush over bread shells. Bake for 10 minutes or till brown and crisp.

3 For filling, shell and devein prawns, coarsely chop. Place in a saucepan with water. Add 2 lemon slices. Bring to boil; reduce heat. Cover; simmer 15 minutes. Strain; reserve liquid.

4 In a saucepan melt butter or margarine. Cook onions in butter till tender. Stir in flour and pepper. Stir in reserved prawn liquid. Cook and stir over medium heat till thickened. Add cream, lemon juice, dillweed, and prawns. Cook and stir till heated through (do not boil).

5 To serve, spoon filling into shells; garnish with dill, lemon peel, and lime slices, if desired.

Cut ¼-inch border around triangles and scoop out centers.

Cook green onions till tender. Stir in flour and pepper.

Add cooked prawns to thickened sauce with cream, lemon juice, and dillweed.

Spoon filling into bread shells just before serving.

Tomato and Olive Flan

A hearty robust dish.

Preparation time:
20 minutes
Chilling time:
30 minutes
Cooking time:
30-35 minutes
Makes 1 flan

PASTRY
2 cups all-purpose flour
1/2 cup butter or margarine, cut into small pieces
2 tablespoons shortening, chilled
1 egg yolk, lightly beaten
2 to 3 tablespoons ice water

FILLING
2 tablespoons olive oil
1 tablespoon Dijon mustard

6 canned anchovy fillets, drained and mashed
1 tablespoon butter
3 small tomatoes, peeled and chopped
2 small onions, thinly sliced
1 cup pitted ripe olives, sliced
2 tablespoons finely chopped fresh basil
1 teaspoon sugar
1 cup shredded Gruyère or Swiss cheese

---

1 Preheat oven to 425°. For pastry, place flour, 1/2 cup butter or margarine, and shortening in a food processor bowl. Cover and process 30 seconds or till mixture has a fine crumbly texture. Combine egg yolk and water and add to flour mixture. Process 30 seconds more or till mixture holds together. Turn out onto a lightly floured surface and knead briefly. Cover with clear plastic wrap; store in refrigerator for 30 minutes.

2 For filling, in bowl or food processor combine oil, mustard, and anchovy fillets. Mash with a fork or process into a smooth paste. Remove pastry from refrigerator and roll out to fit in the bottom and up the sides of a 9-inch flan pan or quiche dish. Carefully place pastry in pan; cover with foil. Spread a layer of dry beans evenly over foil. Bake for 10 to 12 minutes. Remove from oven; remove foil and beans. Cool. Reduce oven temperature to 400°.

3 Spread anchovy mixture over the bottom of the cooled pastry. In a saucepan melt 1 tablespoon butter. Cook tomatoes and onions till tender. Remove from heat and drain off excess liquid. Spoon tomato mixture over anchovy mixture. Combine olives, basil, and sugar and sprinkle over tomato mixture. Sprinkle with cheese.

4 Bake on lowest rack for 20 minutes till pastry is crisp and cheese light brown.

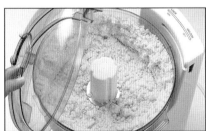

Process flour, butter, and shortening till mixture has a fine crumbly texture.

With floured hands, knead dough briefly on a lightly floured surface.

Spread the anchovy mixture over the bottom of the cooled crust.

Spoon tomato mixture over anchovy mixture before adding olives.

9

Chilled Cod Pâté with Melba Toast

Preparation time:
10 minutes +
chilling
Cooking time:
15 minutes
Serves 4–6

---

1 pound smoked cod
¹/4 cup olive oil
1 clove garlic,
crushed
2 tablespoons all-
purpose flour
1 cup milk

¹/4 cup lemon juice
Melba toast (see
Hint)
Dill sprigs
Lemon slices

---

1 Use a fork to flake the smoked cod and discard any bones.
2 In a large saucepan heat oil. Add flaked fish and garlic and cook for 1 minute. Stir in flour. Add milk. Cook and stir till thickened and bubbly. Cook and stir 1 minute more.

Remove from heat and stir in lemon juice.
3 Pour mixture into a food processor. Cover and process till smooth. Spoon into individual ¹/2-cup serving dishes. Cover and chill till firm. Serve pâté with Melba toast and garnish with dill sprigs and lemon slices.

HINT
Melba toast is available at supermarkets. To make your own, remove the crusts from slices of fresh bread. Flatten with a rolling pin and cut into desired shapes. Dry bread in a 425° oven for 10 minutes. Or, toast slices of white bread on both sides, and remove crusts. Slice through the center with a knife so that each slice is very thin and toasted on one side only. Toast the other side lightly and Cut into desired shapes. Store in an airtight container.

Flake the flesh of the fish with a fork and remove any bones.

Add flour to the fish and garlic mixture in saucepan. Stir over low heat.

Add milk to flour mixture. Cook and stir till thickened and bubbly.

Pour fish mixture into a food processor. Cover and process till smooth.

Ham and Mushroom Gougére

Preparation time:
40 minutes
Cooking time:
40-45 minutes
Serves 4–6

PASTRY
1 cup water
1/3 cup butter or margarine
1 cup all-purpose flour
4 eggs, lightly beaten

FILLING
2 tablespoons butter or margarine
1 onion, chopped
8 ounces mushrooms, sliced

1/4 cup all-purpose flour
3/4 cup chicken broth
8 ounces ham, finely chopped
1 medium tomato, peeled, seeded, and chopped
2 teaspoons Dijon mustard
1 tablespoon chopped fresh basil or thyme

---

1 Preheat oven to 400°. Grease a 2½-quart ovenproof dish. For pastry, in a saucepan heat water and ⅓ cup butter or margarine till boiling; remove from heat and stir in flour. Beat vigorously with a wooden spoon till the flour is thoroughly combined. Cool slightly. Add eggs, a little at a time, beating after each addition. Spread mixture over bottom and up sides of prepared dish.

2 For filling, in a medium saucepan melt 2 tablespoons butter or margarine. Add onion and cook for 1 minute. Add mushrooms; cook till tender and most of the liquid is evaporated. Stir in flour. Add chicken broth. Cook and stir till thickened and bubbly. Cook and stir 1 minute more. Add ham, tomato, mustard, and basil or thyme.

3 Pour filling into pastry shell. Bake, uncovered, 30 minutes. Reduce heat to 350° and bake 10 to 15 minutes or till pastry puffs and browns.

Remove water-butter mixture from heat and vigorously stir in flour.

Add eggs, a little at a time, beating well after each addition.

Stir flour into mushroom mixture. Then add chicken broth.

Add ham, tomato, mustard, and basil to saucepan and stir till well combined.

Cheese Soufflés with Crab Sauce

Preparation time:
35 minutes
Cooking time:
15–20 minutes
Serves 6

¼ cup fine dry bread crumbs
¼ cup butter or margarine
¼ cup all-purpose flour
1 cup milk
½ cup shredded cheddar cheese
¼ cup grated Parmesan cheese
1 teaspoon Dijon mustard
3 eggs, separated

CRAB SAUCE
½ cup butter
3 tablespoons all-purpose flour
1 teaspoon paprika
1 cup chicken broth
½ cup whipping cream
6-ounce can crabmeat, drained, flaked, and cartilage removed
2 tablespoons dry sherry
Freshly ground pepper

---

1 Preheat oven to 350°. Grease six ½-cup individual soufflé dishes or custard cups. Coat bottom and sides with fine dry bread crumbs. Shake off any excess.

2 In a small saucepan melt ¼ cup butter or margarine. Stir in ¼ cup flour. Add milk all at once. Cook and stir till thickened and bubbly. Cook and stir 1 minute more. Remove from heat and stir in cheddar cheese, Parmesan cheese, and mustard till cheese melts. Beat in egg yolks. Transfer mixture to large bowl.

3 In a small clean, dry bowl beat egg whites with an electric mixer till soft peaks form. Fold into cheese mixture. Divide mixture evenly between soufflé dishes. Bake, uncovered, for 10 to 15 minutes or till puffed and golden brown. Serve with Crab Sauce.

4 For Crab Sauce, in a small saucepan melt ½ cup butter. Stir in 3 tablespoons flour and paprika. Add chicken broth and cream all at once. Cook and stir till thickened and bubbly. Cook and stir 1 minute more. Add crab and sherry and season with pepper. Serve immediately.

Note: This soufflé can be baked in a 1-quart soufflé dish for about 45 minutes or till puffed and golden brown. Soufflés are done when they wobble slightly and the center is moist. Soufflés can be made in advance up to Step 2. Cover and chill the cheese mixture and gently reheat it to just warm before adding beaten egg whites.

Coat bottom and sides of soufflé dishes with bread crumbs and shake off excess.

Remove thickened mixture from heat; stir in cheeses and mustard. Beat in yolks.

Place egg whites in a clean dry mixer bowl and beat till soft peaks form.

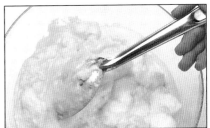

Using a spoon, gradually fold beaten egg whites into cheese mixture.

15

Potato Omelette with Olive Topping

Preparation time:
20 minutes
Cooking time:
10–15 minutes
Serves 4-6

---

*3 slices bacon, finely
  chopped
2 medium potatoes,
  peeled and diced
1 medium onion,
  thinly sliced
6 eggs, lightly beaten
3 tablespoons milk
Freshly ground pepper*

*OLIVE TOPPING
2 x 6¹/₂-ounce cans
  tuna, drained
¹/₂ cup pitted ripe
  olives
¹/₄ cup olive oil
¹/₄ cup lemon juice
1 tablespoon drained
  capers
¹/₂ cup chopped parsley
Lemon slices
Fresh thyme*

---

1 In a large skillet cook bacon till crisp. Drain on paper towels, reserving bacon drippings. Cook potato in skillet with bacon drippings till brown; remove from skillet. Add onion to skillet and cook till tender. Return bacon and potatoes to pan.
2 In a bowl combine eggs and milk. Pour in skillet over potato mixture. Season with pepper. Cover skillet and cook over low heat for 10 to 15 minutes or till set.
3 For Olive Topping, place tuna, olives, olive oil, lemon juice, and capers in a food processor. Cover and process till smooth.
4 To serve, spread omelette with topping and sprinkle with parsley. Garnish with lemon slices and thyme, if desired. Cut into wedges to serve.

Note: The Olive Topping is called Tapenade in France and is often served with hard-cooked eggs as an appetizer. Try it spread on crackers or toast.

Add potatoes to the pan and cook, stirring often, till brown.

Return cooked bacon to pan with onion mixture.

Pour egg mixture over bacon and potato mixture.

Process tuna, olives, olive oil, lemon juice, and capers.

Leek Tart

Serve piping hot.

Preparation time:
30 minutes + standing
Cooking time:
30–40 minutes
Makes 1 flan

PASTRY
*2 cups all-purpose
flour*
*1/2 cup butter or
margarine, cut into
small pieces*
*2 tablespoons
shortening, chilled*
*2 tablespoons lemon
juice*
*2 to 3 tablespoons ice
water*

FILLING
*2 slices bacon, finely
chopped*
*5 leeks, cleaned and
thinly sliced*
*1/3 cup all-purpose
flour*
1 cup milk
*2 eggs, lightly
beaten*
*1 cup shredded
cheddar cheese*
1/2 teaspoon pepper
1 beaten egg

---

1 Preheat oven to 400°. **For pastry,** place 2 cups flour, 1/2 cup butter or margarine, and shortening in a food processor. Cover and process till mixture has a fine crumbly texture. Add lemon juice and water. Process 30 seconds more or till smooth. Wrap in clear plastic wrap and chill for 30 minutes.

2 For filling, in a medium skillet cook bacon till crisp. Add leeks and cook for 5 minutes or till tender. Stir in 1/3 cup flour. Add milk. Cook and stir till thickened and bubbly. Cook and stir 1 minute more. Cool slightly. Stir in 2 eggs, cheese, and pepper.

3 Roll 2/3 of the pastry out to fit in the bottom and up the sides of a 9-inch flan pan or quiche dish. Place pastry in pan. Spoon filling over pastry. Roll out remaining pastry to cover top of pie. Trim, seal, and flute edges. Brush with 1 beaten egg. Cut three deep slits in top of pastry to allow steam to escape. Bake, uncovered, for 30 to 40 minutes or till pastry is golden and crisp. Cut into wedges to serve.

HINT
Leeks have a mild onion flavor and when they are cooked slowly in butter, develop a creamy texture. The white part of the leek is the most tender, but you can use about 2-inches of the green. The rest will be too tough and fibrous. Leeks require thorough washing before using. Slit into the fleshy parts and cut almost to the base. This loosens the layers so that soil can be easily removed when rinsed under running water.

Process flour, butter, and shortening till mixture is crumbly.

Roll out two-thirds of the pastry to fit in the bottom and up the sides of pan.

Add leeks to bacon in pan. Cook for 5 minutes or till leeks are tender.

Spoon the slightly cooled filling over pastry.

19

Place lemon slices, onion, garlic, and thyme into clean fish cavity.

Score the thickest part of the fish with two diagonal slashes on both sides.

Stir in tomatoes, wine, lemon juice, anchovies, sugar, and thyme.

Pour sauce over fish in baking dish and bake about 50 minutes.

SEAFOOD

French seafood dishes usually come with a sauce, either cooked with the fish or poured over. It helps keep the seafood moist.

Baked Snapper with Garlic and Tomatoes

Preparation time:
  25 minutes
Cooking time:
  40–50 minutes
Serves 4–6

2- to 3-pound drawn red snapper (see Hint)
3 slices lemon
1 small onion, thickly sliced
1 clove garlic
1 sprig fresh thyme
1 tablespoon olive oil

SAUCE
3 tablespoons olive oil
1 clove garlic, crushed
1 small onion, chopped

14¹/₂-ounce can chopped tomatoes, undrained
²/₃ cup dry white wine
¹/₃ cup lemon juice
2 canned anchovy fillets, mashed
1 teaspoon sugar
1 sprig fresh thyme
Fresh thyme for garnish (optional)
Lemon slices (optional)

1 Preheat oven to 400°. Rinse fish and pat dry with paper towels. Place lemon slices, onion, garlic clove, and 1 sprig of thyme into cavity of fish. With a sharp knife score the thickest part of the fish with two diagonal slashes. Turn fish over and score other side. Rub outside of fish with olive oil. Place fish in a baking dish.
2 For sauce, in a saucepan heat oil. Cook chopped onion and garlic in hot oil till tender. Stir in undrained tomatoes, white wine, lemon juice, anchovies, sugar, and sprig of thyme. Bring to a boil; reduce heat. Simmer, uncovered, till sauce is reduced by one-third and slightly thickened.
3 Pour sauce over fish in baking dish. Bake, uncovered, for 40 to 50 minutes or till fish flakes easily when tested with a fork. Garnish with fresh thyme and lemon slices, if desired.

HINT
A drawn fish is a whole fish minus its internal organs. A drawn fish may still need to be scaled. To scale the fish, grasp wet fish by the tail with one hand. With the other hand, use a scaler or dull knife to scrape from the tail to the head using short, swift strokes. Rinse and pat dry.

Fish Fillets with Butter Sauce

Preparation time:
30 minutes
Cooking time:
30-40 minutes
Serves 4

1 1/2–2 pounds
  whitefish fillets
1/3 cup all-purpose
  flour
Freshly ground
  pepper
1/4 cup butter
1 cup fish stock or
  chicken broth
1/4 cup lemon juice
2 egg yolks
1/3 cup whipping
  cream

1/2 cup chopped
  parsley
Lemon (optional)
Lime (optional)

FISH STOCK
6 ounces fish
  trimmings (see Note)
1 3/4 cups water
1/2 cup dry white wine
6 peppercorns
2 slices lemon
Parsley stems
1 bay leaf

1 Rinse fish and pat dry with paper towels. Cut fish into four portions. Season flour with pepper; toss fish lightly in flour mixture. Shake off any excess.
2 In a large skillet melt butter. When butter is golden brown, add fish fillets. Cook over medium-high heat for 1 minute on each side. Drain on paper towels.
3 Stir any remaining flour into the pan juices. Add stock and lemon juice. Cook and stir till thickened and bubbly. Add fish and simmer, uncovered, for 5 to 10 minutes or till fish flakes easily with a fork. Remove fish and keep warm. Combine egg yolks and cream and add to the sauce. Cook and stir till thickened (do not boil). Serve sauce over fish. Garnish with lemon and lime slices and sprinkle with parsley, if desired.
4 For stock, in a large saucepan combine fish trimmings, water, wine, peppercorns, lemon, parsley stems, and bay leaf. Bring to a boil; reduce heat. Simmer, uncovered, for 20 minutes. Strain. Measure stock and add enough water, if necessary, to make 1 cup liquid.

Note: Fish trimmings are available from your grocer's fresh fish case.

HINT
Before cooking the fillets, the butter must be golden brown—this gives the fish a characteristic "nutty" flavor. Fish stock should only be cooked for 20 minutes. Beef and chicken stock require long cooking to extract the flavor but fish stock is quick to make. Make sure your fish trimmings are from white-fleshed, low-fat fish such as cod, flounder or halibut.

When the butter is golden brown, add fish and cook for 1 minute on each side.

Add flour to pan juices and stir till well combined.

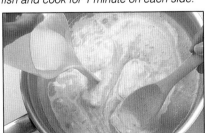

Stir egg yolk and cream mixture into the sauce and heat gently.

Garnish the fish with thin slices of lemon and lime.

Trout with Almonds

Preparation time:
15 minutes
Cooking time:
15 minutes
Serves 4

4 drawn lake trout (about 6 ounces each) (whole fish minus internal organs)	*Freshly ground pepper*
1/3 cup all-purpose flour	*1/3 cup lemon juice*
1/2 teaspoon dried dillweed	*1/3 cup butter or margarine*
1/4 teaspoon dry mustard	*1/2 cup blanched almonds, halved crosswise*
	1/2 cup dry white wine
	Fresh dill (optional)

1 Using scissors, remove fins from trout and trim tail. Rinse fish and pat dry with paper towels. Stir together flour, dillweed, and mustard; season with pepper.

2 Brush surface of fish with lemon juice, reserving any excess juice. Coat whole trout in seasoned flour mixture. Shake off any excess.

3 In a large skillet cook butter or margarine and almonds till golden. Remove almonds with a slotted spoon and drain almonds on paper towels. Add fish to skillet and cook over medium-high heat till fish flakes easily when tested with a fork, carefully turning fish once. Drain on paper towels.

4 Add remaining lemon juice to skillet with drippings. Stir in wine. Bring to a boil. Cook over high heat until reduced by half. Stir in reserved almonds and pour over fish at once. Garnish with fresh dill, if desired.

Using scissors, remove the fins and trim the tail from the trout.

Coat trout in flour seasoned with dill, mustard, and pepper to form a crust.

Cook fish over medium-high heat till fish flakes easily with a fork, turning once.

Simmer lemon juice and wine in skillet over high heat until it is reduced by half.

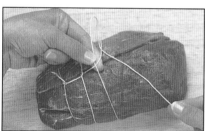

Tie the meat with string to help hold its shape during cooking.

Add meat to oil in pan and brown quickly on all sides to seal in juices.

Spread the top surface of the cooled meat with pâté.

Place meat, pâté side down, on middle of pastry. Brush edges with egg and seal.

MEAT & POULTRY

The French make the most of meat and poultry, using not only the expensive cuts, but the cheaper ones too, in casseroles and stews.

Beef Fillet in Pastry Crust with Horseradish Cream

Preparation time:
20 minutes
Cooking time:
30 minutes
Serves 6

1¹/2 pounds beef tenderloin
2 cloves garlic, crushed
¹/4 cup olive oil
1 teaspoon ground pepper
3¹/2 ounces purchased chicken, mushroom, or vegetarian pâté (about ²/3 cup)
¹/2 of a 17¹/2-ounce package (1 sheet) frozen puff pastry, thawed
1 beaten egg

SAUCE
1 cup sour cream
1 tablespoon prepared horseradish (see Note)
1 tablespoon chopped chives
Freshly ground pepper

---

1 Preheat oven to 400°. Trim meat of excess fat. Tie meat with string to hold its shape during cooking. Rub the surface of the meat with garlic, 1 tablespoon of the oil, and pepper.

2 In a large skillet heat remaining oil. Add meat and brown on all sides over high heat about 5 minutes. Set aside to cool. Remove string when cool.

3 On a lightly floured surface roll pastry into a rectangle large enough to encase the meat. Spread top of cooled meat with pâté. Place meat, pâté side down, on middle of pastry. Brush edges of pastry with egg; seal around meat.

4 Place meat in shallow baking pan, pâté side up. Brush with egg and decorate with pastry cut-outs, if desired. Bake, uncovered, for 35 minutes or till pastry is golden brown and meat medium-rare. Let stand 10 minutes.

5 For sauce, in a bowl stir together sour cream, horseradish, and chives. Serve in a small serving bowl with the meat.

Note: If horseradish is unavailable, add 2 tablespoons Dijon mustard to the cream as a substitute.

Beef and Red Wine Casserole

Preparation time:
25 minutes
Cooking time:
1½ hours
Serves 6

1½ pounds round steak	*2 cups dry red wine*
4 slices Canadian bacon	*1 tablespoon prepared horseradish*
2 tablespoons olive oil	*1 teaspoon fresh thyme leaves*
12 small white onions, peeled	*2 tablespoons butter*
2 cloves garlic, crushed	*12 ounces mushrooms*
¼ cup all-purpose flour	*Fresh thyme*

1 Trim meat of excess fat; cut into ½-inch cubes. Cut bacon into ¼-inch strips.

2 In a large saucepan heat oil. Add bacon and cook till brown. Drain on paper towel and reserve drippings. Cook meat in hot drippings over medium high heat till brown. Remove from pan. Add whole onions and cook over medium high heat till brown. Add garlic and cook for 1 minute. Return meat to pan. Stir in flour. Add red wine, horseradish, and thyme. Cook and stir till thickened and bubbly. Return onions and bacon to pan. Cover; simmer for 1 hour.

3 Meanwhile, in a medium saucepan melt butter. Cook mushrooms in butter till tender. Add mushrooms to meat mixture. Cook, uncovered, for 30 minutes more.

4 Garnish each serving with fresh thyme and serve with crusty French bread.

HINT
Domestic rabbit can be used in place of beef in this recipe. Store the cooked casserole overnight in the refrigerator to allow flavors to develop more fully.

Cut beef into ½-inch cubes. Cut bacon into ¼-inch strips.

Heat oil in saucepan and cook bacon till brown.

Add red wine, horseradish, and thyme to saucepan. Cook and stir till thickened.

Thirty minutes before serving, add cooked mushrooms to meat mixture.

Pepper Steak

Preparation time:
15 minutes
Cooking time:
15 minutes
Serves 6

6 beef top loin or tenderloin steaks, cut 1 inch thick (about 2 pounds)	*1 cup beef broth*
3 tablespoons butter	*1/3 cup dry sherry or brandy*
1 onion, chopped	*1/2 cup whipping cream*
1 clove garlic, crushed	*2 tablespoons bottled green peppercorns*
3 tablespoons all-purpose flour	*Parsley*

1 Trim meat of excess fat. In a large skillet heat butter. Add onion and garlic and cook over medium heat for 1 minute. Increase heat to high and brown steaks 2 minutes on each side; remove from pan. Remove pan from heat and stir in flour. Return pan to heat and cook and stir till flour browns.

2 Add beef broth and sherry to skillet. Cook and stir till thickened. Cook and stir 1 minute more. Add cream and peppercorns, crushing peppercorns lightly with a spoon.

3 Return steaks to sauce and cook 7 to 12 minutes more or till done as desired.

Add steaks to onion mixture and brown over high heat 2 minutes on each side.

Stir flour into pan juices. Return to heat and cook and stir till flour browns.

Add cream and peppercorns to sauce,
crushing peppercorns with a spoon.

Return steaks to sauce and cook for 7 to
12 minutes more or till desired doneness.

Cassoulet

Preparation time:
25 minutes
Cooking time:
1½ hours
Serves 6

---

8 ounces boneless skinless chicken thighs	*14½-ounce can chopped tomatoes, undrained*
8 ounces lean boneless lamb	*1 cup dry white wine*
8 ounces lean boneless pork	*1 teaspoon fresh thyme leaves*
¼ cup lard or butter	*2 bay leaves*
2 medium onions, chopped	*3 cloves*
2 cloves garlic, crushed	*Freshly ground pepper*
2 stalks celery, chopped	*16-ounce can white cannellini beans, drained*
1 tablespoon all-purpose flour	*4 ounces salami, chopped*

1 Trim meat of excess fat and cut into ¾-inch cubes. In saucepan heat lard or butter. Cook chicken in hot pan 2 to 3 minutes till brown; remove. Cook lamb 2 to 3 minutes or till brown; remove. Cook pork 2 to 3 minutes or till brown; remove.

2 Add onions to fat in pan; cook till tender and brown. Add garlic and celery; cook and stir 1 minute. Stir in flour. Add tomatoes and wine. Cook and stir till thickened. Cook and stir for 1 minute more. Add thyme, bay leaves, and cloves; season with pepper. Bring to boil; reduce heat. Simmer, uncovered, 10 minutes.

3 Add browned poultry and meat and cannellini beans to pan. Cover and simmer for 1 hour or till meat is tender. Add salami. Cover and simmer for 30 minutes more. Remove and discard bay leaves.

Trim chicken, lamb, and pork of excess fat and cut into ¾-inch cubes.

Add lamb to saucepan. Cook and stir till brown and remove from pan.

Add thyme, bay leaves, cloves, and pepper to the thickened sauce.

Add browned meat and poultry and cannellini beans to sauce.

Pork with Cabbage and Plums

Preparation time:
30 minutes
Cooking time:
1½– 1¾ hours
Serves 4–6

2-pound boneless pork loin roast (single loin)	*SAUCE*
2 tablespoons butter, softened	*30-ounce can whole, purple plums*
1 teaspoon ground allspice	*2 tablespoons butter*
½ cup water	*4 green onions, finely chopped*
2 tablespoons butter	*⅓ cup red wine vinegar*
1 large onion, thinly sliced	*1 teaspoon instant chicken bouillon granules*
1 pound cabbage, shredded	*¼ cup all-purpose flour*
⅓ cup lemon juice	*1 cup chicken broth*

1 Preheat oven to 350°. Trim pork of excess fat. Tie securely with a string. In a small bowl stir together 2 tablespoons softened butter and allspice till well combined; spread over pork. Place meat on a rack in a roasting pan. Insert meat thermometer. Pour water into pan. Roast for 1½ to 1¾ hours or till meat thermometer registers 160°. Let stand 10 minutes.

2 In a large saucepan heat 2 tablespoons butter. Add onion and cook till tender and brown. Stir in cabbage. Add lemon juice. Cover and simmer for 10 to 15 minutes or till cabbage is tender. Set aside; keep warm.

3 For sauce, drain plums, reserving syrup. Place plums in an ovenproof dish; set aside. In a saucepan heat 2 tablespoons butter. Cook green onions in butter over medium heat for 1 minute; add vinegar and cook 1 minute more. Add plum syrup and bouillon granules to pan. Bring to a boil; reduce heat. Simmer, uncovered, 5 minutes; set aside. Warm plums in 300° oven for 15 minutes before serving.

4 Remove meat from pan, reserving drippings for gravy. Thinly slice meat; keep warm. Measure ⅓ cup of drippings. Transfer drippings to a skillet. Stir in flour. Cook and stir till flour browns. Add chicken broth and plum syrup mixture. Cook and stir till thickened. Cook and stir for 1 minute more.

5 To serve, arrange cabbage on a serving plate and overlap pork slices down center. Arrange warm plums around meat; pour small amount of gravy over meat. Pass remaining gravy.

Stir together softened butter and allspice till well combined.

Spread butter mixture over securely tied pork.

Add shredded cabbage to onion mixture in pan.

Add plum syrup and bouillon granules to pan.

Veal with Dijon Mustard Sauce

Preparation time:
  15 minutes
Cooking time:
  20 minutes
Serves 6

---

6 veal top round steaks or boneless sirloin steaks
1/4 cup all-purpose flour
Freshly ground pepper
2 tablespoons butter or margarine
2 slices Canadian bacon, chopped

1 large onion, chopped
1 cup dry white wine
2/3 cup chicken broth
1/2 cup light cream
1/4 cup Dijon mustard
1 teaspoon fresh thyme leaves or 1/4 teaspoon dried thyme, crushed
Fresh dill

---

1 Trim meat of excess fat. In a bowl combine flour and pepper. Coat veal steaks in flour mixture, reserving any excess flour. In a large skillet melt butter or margarine. Cook bacon and onion in butter till bacon is crisp and onion is tender and brown. Remove from pan. Add veal to hot skillet and cook for 1 minute on each side or till brown.

Remove from pan.
2 Stir remaining flour into pan drippings. Add wine and chicken broth. Cook and stir till thickened and bubbly. Cook and stir 1 minute more. Return bacon and onion to pan. Stir in cream, mustard, and thyme. Return steaks to sauce and gently simmer, uncovered, about 5 minutes or till tender. Garnish each serving with fresh dill.

Note: Dijon mustard is an aromatic mustard from the French town of Dijon. It is perfect for this recipe because its mild flavor does not overpower the delicate veal.

Add bacon and onion to hot butter in pan. Cook till golden brown.

Add meat to hot skillet and brown on both sides. Remove from pan.

Stir cream, mustard, and thyme into
thickened mixture.

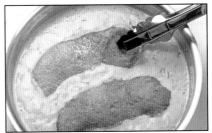

Return steaks to sauce and simmer
about 5 minutes or till tender.

Lamb Navarin (Lamb Casserole with Vegetables)

Preparation time:
20 minutes
Cooking time:
1 – 1½ hours
Serves 6

2 pounds lamb leg chops
¼ cup olive oil
2 tablespoons butter
2 medium onions, chopped
2 parsnips, chopped
2 carrots, chopped
2 stalks celery, chopped
1 clove garlic, crushed
¼ cup all-purpose flour
14½-ounce can chopped tomatoes, undrained

1 cup chicken broth
⅔ cup water
⅔ cup frozen cut green beans
½ cup chopped parsley
2 tablespoons chopped fresh mint
1 teaspoon fresh thyme leaves
Freshly ground pepper
1 tablespoon Dijon mustard
Hot cooked noodles

1   Preheat oven to 300°. Trim meat of excess fat and bones and cut into ¾-inch cubes. In a large saucepan heat oil and butter. Brown half of the meat in hot pan. Remove from pan and drain on paper towels. Brown remaining meat; remove from pan and drain on paper towels.

2   Cook onions in pan till tender and brown. Stir in parsnips, carrots, celery, and garlic. Cook and stir till vegetables are tender. Stir in flour. Add tomatoes, chicken broth, and water. Cook and stir till thickened and bubbly. Stir in frozen beans, parsley, mint, and thyme. Add meat.

3   Transfer mixture to a casserole. Cover and cook for 1 to 1½ hours or till lamb is tender. Serve with noodles.

Trim meat of excess fat and bones and cut into ³/4-inch cubes.

Brown meat, half at a time, in hot oil and butter. Drain on paper towels.

Add parsnips, carrots, celery, and garlic to cooked onions. Cook till tender.

Add browned meat to sauce. Transfer to casserole; cook in oven for 1–1½ hours.

Roast Chicken with Grapes

A late summer dish.

Preparation time:
25 minutes
Standing time:
15 minutes
Cooking time:
1½ hours
Serves 4–6

---

1 cup boiling water
1 cup bulgur
½ cup chopped
parsley
¼ cup chopped chives
1 tablespoon finely
shredded lemon peel
2 tablespoons lemon
juice
1 teaspoon dried
tarragon, crushed
2 cup seedless white
grapes, halved
3 tablespoons butter
or margarine
1 egg, lightly beaten

Freshly ground
pepper
3-pound whole chicken
2 teaspoons paprika

SAUCE
¼ cup all-purpose
flour
1 cup chicken broth
½ cup dry white wine
3 cups seedless white
grapes, halved
Freshly ground
pepper
½ cup whipping
cream

---

1 Preheat oven to 350°. In a bowl pour boiling water over bulgur. Let stand 15 minutes. Drain off excess water. Stir in parsley, chives, lemon peel, lemon juice, and tarragon. Add 2 cups grapes, 2 tablespoons of the butter or margarine, and egg. Season with pepper.

2 Rinse chicken and pat dry with paper towels. Spoon bulgur mixture into cavity. Tie wings and legs together with string to secure bulgur mixture. Place chicken on rack in a shallow roasting pan. Spread with remaining butter and sprinkle with paprika.

3 Bake, uncovered, for 1¼ to 1½ hours or till no pink remains and juices run clear. Remove from pan. Cover with foil and let stand 10 minutes.

4 For sauce, drain fat from pan, reserving ¼ cup. Place reserved drippings in saucepan and stir in flour. Cook and stir till flour browns. Stir in chicken broth and wine. Cook and stir till thickened and bubbly. Cook and stir 1 minute more. Add 3 cups grapes and season with pepper. Simmer, uncovered, for 5 minutes. Add cream just before serving. Heat through.

5 To serve, remove bulgur from chicken. Cut chicken into pieces and arrange on a serving platter with bulgur. Pour sauce over chicken.

HINT
Roast chicken and meats should stand for 10 to 15 minutes before carving. This makes the meat easier to cut and prevents loss of juices.

Add beaten egg to other stuffing ingredients and stir till well combined.

Spoon stuffing into clean chicken cavity.

Add chicken broth and wine to browned flour mixture. Cook and stir till thick.

Add grapes to sauce and season with pepper. Simmer for 5 minutes more.

Tarragon Cream Chicken

Preparation time:
   15 minutes
Cooking time:
   15 minutes
Serves 4

4 boneless skinless chicken breasts	*1 cup dry white wine*
¼ cup all-purpose flour	*1 cup chicken broth*
Freshly ground pepper	*1½ teaspoons dried tarragon, crushed*
¼ cup butter	*⅓ cup whipping cream*
2 leeks, chopped	*Fresh tarragon*

1 Rinse chicken and pat dry. Combine flour and pepper. Coat chicken in flour mixture. Reserve remaining flour. In skillet melt butter. Add chicken. Cook 2 to 3 minutes on each side or till brown. Remove from skillet. 2 Add leeks to skillet and cook till tender. Stir in remaining flour. Add wine and broth. Cook and stir till thickened. Cook and stir 1 minute. Add dried tarragon; simmer, uncovered, for 5 minutes. 3 Return chicken to skillet. Simmer, uncovered, 10 minutes or till no longer pink. Stir in cream just before serving. Heat through. Garnish with tarragon.

Toss chicken in mixture of flour and pepper.

Cook chicken in hot butter over medium heat till brown on both sides.

Add remaining flour to leek mixture in skillet.

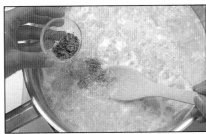

Add tarragon to sauce and simmer, uncovered, for 5 minutes.

43

Chicken with Peppers

Preparation time:
25 minutes
Cooking time:
20 minutes
Serves 6

---

2 pounds boneless skinless chicken thighs	*2 small red bell peppers, thinly sliced*
4 slices bacon, finely chopped	*¼ cup all-purpose flour*
2 large onions, thinly sliced	*4 small ripe tomatoes, seeded and chopped*
2 cloves garlic, crushed	*1 cup chicken broth*
2 small green bell peppers, thinly sliced	*2 tablespoons red wine vinegar*
	1 tablespoon sugar
	Hot cooked rice
	Fresh thyme

---

1 Rinse chicken and pat dry with paper towels. Trim thighs of excess fat and cut thighs in half. In a large skillet cook bacon till crisp. Drain on paper towels, reserving drippings. Add chicken to hot skillet. Cook for 2 to 3 minutes on each side or till brown. Remove from skillet. Cook onion and garlic in skillet till onion is tender and brown. Add bell peppers and cook 5 minutes more.

2 Stir flour into skillet. Return bacon to pan. Add tomatoes, chicken broth, vinegar, and sugar. Cook and stir till thickened and bubbly. Reduce heat and simmer, uncovered, 10 minutes. Transfer to a large saucepan.

3 Add chicken pieces to pepper mixture in pan. Simmer, uncovered, 10 minutes or till chicken is tender. Serve with rice; garnish with thyme.

Note: Tomatoes don't have to be peeled for this dish but they should be seeded. Cut tomato in half and gently squeeze out seeds. Any seeds that remain can be removed with a small spoon.

Trim chicken thighs of excess fat and cut in half.

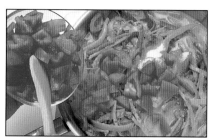

Cook onion and garlic till brown and add bell peppers.

Add tomatoes, chicken broth, vinegar, and sugar to skillet mixture.

Add chicken to sauce and simmer for 10 minutes or till no longer pink.

Break watercress into small sprigs, discarding the coarser stems.

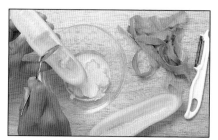

Peel cucumber and halve lengthwise. Use a spoon to scrape out seeds.

VEGETABLES

Often the French serve vegetables and salads as a course on their own. All of these dishes can be served on their own, as a first course or a light meal.

Watercress Salad

A tart tasting salad.

Preparation time:
35 minutes
Cooking time:
None
Serves 4–6

---

3 cups loosely packed watercress	*DRESSING*
3 stalks celery	*¼ cup olive oil*
1 cucumber	*¼ cup lemon juice*
3 medium oranges	*1 tablespoon honey*
1 red onion, sliced and separated into rings	*2 teaspoons finely shredded orange peel*
¼ cup chopped chives	*1 teaspoon coarse grain mustard*
½ cup chopped pecans or walnuts	*Freshly ground pepper*

---

1 Rinse watercress and pat dry. Break into small sprigs, discarding stems. Cut celery into 2-inch strips. Peel cucumber and halve lengthwise. Using a spoon, scrape out cucumber seeds. Cut into 2-inch strips.

Peel oranges and cut into sections. Cover oranges and chill till serving time.

2 For dressing, in a screw top jar combine oil, lemon juice, honey, orange peel, mustard, and pepper. Cover and shake till well combined. Chill till serving time.

3 To serve, in a bowl combine watercress, celery, cucumber, onion, and chives. Pour dressing over, tossing to coat. Add oranges; toss gently to coat. Sprinkle with nuts.

Peel oranges, being careful to remove all of the white pith.

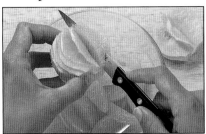

Cut orange into sections by cutting between the membrane and flesh.

Beans with Tomatoes

Preparation time:
10 minutes
Cooking time:
15 minutes
Serves 6

1 pound fresh green beans	*2 tablespoons red wine vinegar*
14¹/₂-ounce can whole tomatoes	*¹/₄ cup chopped pitted ripe olives*
2 tablespoons olive oil	*1 tablespoon chopped fresh basil*
1 large onion, chopped	*Freshly ground pepper*
1 clove garlic, crushed	*Fresh basil*
2 teaspoons sugar	

1 Trim beans and cut into 2-inch pieces. Cook in boiling water for 5 minutes. Drain, rinse with cold water. Set aside. Drain and chop tomatoes, reserving juice.

2 In a large skillet heat oil. Add onion and garlic and cook till onion is tender and brown. Sprinkle with sugar; cook and stir till sugar caramelizes. Add vinegar; cook 1 minute. Add tomatoes and juice, olives, basil, and pepper. Bring to a boil; reduce heat. Simmer, uncovered, for 5 minutes.

3 Add beans. Simmer, uncovered, for 10 minutes. Place on serving platter. Garnish with basil.

Trim ends of beans and cut into 2-inch pieces.

Drain tomatoes, reserving their juice. Chop tomatoes.

Add tomatoes and juice, olives, basil, and pepper to onion mixture.

Add partially-cooked beans to tomato mixture and simmer for 10 minutes.

Potato Cake

Serve with salad.

Preparation time:
20 minutes
Cooking time:
1 hour
Serves 4–6

8 medium potatoes	*1 cup shredded*
2 tablespoons butter	*mozzarella or*
2 tablespoons olive oil	*cheddar cheese*
1 clove garlic, crushed	*1/2 cup grated*
1/2 teaspoon pepper	*Parmesan cheese*
2 cups fine dry bread	*Parsley*
crumbs	

1 Preheat oven to 350°. Grease an 8-inch springform pan. Line base and sides of pan with waxed paper.
2 Peel potatoes and thinly slice. In a small saucepan heat butter, oil, garlic, and pepper. Arrange some of the potato slices in bottom of pan, overlapping edges. Brush with butter mixture. Combine bread crumbs and cheeses; sprinkle some over potato slices. Continue layering potatoes, brushing with butter mixture and sprinkling with cheese mixture, ending with cheese. Using your hand, press the top layer down.
3 Bake, uncovered, 1 hour or until golden brown. Cool slightly, cut into wedges. Serve warm.

Peel potatoes and thinly slice with a sharp knife or in a food processor.

Arrange some of the potato slices in bottom of pan, overlapping edges.

Sprinkle each layer with bread crumb and cheese mixture.

Using your hand, firmly press the top layer down.

Ratatouille (Eggplant & Tomato Casserole)

Preparation time:
30 minutes
Standing time:
30 minutes
Cooking time:
45 minutes
Serves 4–6

2 medium eggplant (about 1 pound each)
Salt
1/2 cup olive oil
1 large onion, chopped
2 cloves garlic, crushed
2 medium zucchini, cut into 1/4-inch slices

2 tablespoons red wine vinegar
2 teaspoons sugar
Freshly ground pepper
2 medium ripe tomatoes, peeled, seeded, and chopped
1/4 cup dry white wine
1/4 cup grated Parmesan cheese

1 Cut eggplant into 1/2-inch slices. Sprinkle lightly with salt. Place in a colander and let stand 30 minutes. Wash salt off eggplant and pat dry with paper towels.
2 In a large skillet heat oil. Add onion and cook till tender and brown. Add eggplant slices and garlic to onion mixture and cook till eggplant is brown, turning eggplant once. Remove from skillet.

Add zucchini and cook till brown.
3 Transfer all vegetables to saucepan. Add vinegar, sugar, and pepper. Stir in tomatoes and wine. Bring to boil; reduce heat. Cover; simmer 30 minutes. Sprinkle with Parmesan cheese before serving.

HINT

This casserole may be served hot or cold. It can be served alone with French bread or as an accompaniment to meat or poultry dishes. Eggplant can taste bitter, depending on its size and age. Salting eggplant and letting it stand about 30 minutes draws out these bitter juices. Rinse well before cooking.

Cut eggplant into 1/2-inch slices and sprinkle with salt.

Add eggplant and garlic to onion mixture and cook till brown on both sides.

Add vinegar, sugar, and pepper to vegetables in saucepan.

Add tomatoes and wine and simmer, covered, for 30 minutes.

Potato Puffs

Light and fluffy.

Preparation time:
30 minutes
Cooking time:
15 minutes
Serves 6

3 medium potatoes	*2 green onions, chopped*
1 cup water	*1/2 teaspoon ground*
3 tablespoons butter	*nutmeg*
1 cup all-purpose flour	*Oil for deep-fat*
2 eggs, lightly beaten	*frying*
1 cup shredded Gruyere	
or Swiss cheese	

1 Peel and quarter potatoes. Cook, covered, in boiling salted water for 20 minutes or till tender. Drain and mash.
2 In a saucepan combine water and butter. Bring to a boil. Add flour and stir vigorously. Cook and stir till mixture forms a ball. Remove from heat. Cool 5 minutes. Add eggs, a little at a time, beating well with a wooden spoon after each till smooth. Stir in mashed potatoes, cheese, onions, and nutmeg.
3 Drop dough by heaping tablespoons into hot oil (375°). Cook 3 to 4 minutes or till golden brown, turning once. Drain on paper towels. Serve immediately.

Add flour all at once to butter and water mixture and stir vigorously.

Allow mixture to cool slightly, then beat in eggs, a little at a time.

Stir mashed potatoes, shredded cheese, onions, and nutmeg into egg mixture.

Deep-fry tablespoonsful of the dough in hot oil till puffed and golden brown.

Remove core from peeled and quartered apples and brush with lemon juice.

Add cream and vanilla to the egg and flour mixture.

Arrange apple over pastry and sprinkle with powdered sugar and cinnamon.

Pour egg mixture over partially-baked apples and bake 1 hour longer or till set.

DESSERTS

Fresh fruit is best served at the end of a really rich meal. But for those special occasions, here are four spectacular French desserts.

French Apple Flan

Preparation time:
45 minutes
Chilling time:
30 minutes
Cooking time:
1 1/2 hours
Makes 1 flan

ALMOND PASTRY
1 1/2 cups all-purpose flour
1/2 cup ground almonds
2 tablespoons sugar
1/2 cup unsalted butter
3 tablespoons shortening, chilled
5 to 6 tablespoons ice water

FILLING
3 medium Granny Smith or golden delicious apples

2 tablespoons lemon juice
2 eggs, lightly beaten
2 tablespoons all-purpose flour
3/4 cup milk or light cream
1 teaspoon vanilla
1/4 cup sifted powdered sugar
1/4 teaspoon ground cinnamon

1 Preheat oven to 400°. Grease a 9-inch deep flan pan and lightly coat with flour. For pastry, in a food processor combine 1 1/2 cups flour, almonds, butter, shortening, and sugar. Cover and process for 30 seconds or till mixture has a fine crumbly texture. Add water and process till smooth. Wrap dough in plastic wrap and chill for 30 minutes. 2 For filling, peel, quarter, and core apples; brush with lemon juice. In a medium bowl combine eggs and flour with a wire whisk. Add milk or cream and vanilla; whisk till well combined. 3 On a lightly floured surface roll pastry till about 1/8-inch thick. Place in flan pan, pressing pastry onto bottom and up sides of the pan. Arrange apple quarters over bottom of pastry. Sprinkle with sugar and cinnamon. Bake, uncovered, 30 minutes. Remove from oven; pour egg mixture over apples. Reduce heat to 300°. Bake for 1 hour further or till set.

Crêpes Suzette

Preparation time:
30 minutes
Cooking time:
35 minutes
Serves 4–6

CRÊPE BATTER
1 cup all-purpose
  flour
1 cup milk
2 eggs, lightly beaten
1 tablespoon sugar
1 tablespoon butter,
  melted
1 tablespoon brandy

SAUCE
1/4 cup butter

1/4 cup sugar
1 tablespoon finely
  shredded orange peel
1 tablespoon finely
  shredded lemon peel
1 cup orange juice
1/2 cup Grand
  Marnier
1/4 cup lemon juice
Whipped cream or ice
  cream

---

1 For batter, in a food processor combine flour, milk, eggs, sugar, 1 tablespoon butter, and brandy. Cover and process till smooth. Transfer to a bowl; cover with plastic wrap. Let stand 1 hour or till batter is the consistency of light cream. If the batter thickens too much, thin with milk or water.

2 To cook crêpes, heat a lightly greased 6-inch skillet. Remove from heat. Spoon in 2 tablespoons of the batter, lifting and tilting the skillet to spread batter. Return to heat and brown one side. Flip crêpe and lightly brown other side. Invert pan over plate; remove crêpe. Repeat with remaining batter, greasing skillet occasionally.

3 For sauce, in a saucepan combine 1/4 cup butter and sugar. Cook and stir over medium heat till sugar turns golden brown. Stir in orange peel, lemon peel, orange juice, Grand Marnier, and lemon juice. Bring to a boil; reduce heat. Simmer, uncovered, 10 minutes.

4 To serve, preheat oven to 400°. Fold crêpes into quarters and arrange in the bottom of an ovenproof dish, overlapping edges. Pour sauce over crêpes. Bake, uncovered, for 10 minutes. Serve warm with whipped cream or ice cream.

HINT

Crêpes can be flambéed at the table, but be extremely careful. Heat 2 tablespoons Grand Marnier, brandy, or orange liqueur in a small saucepan. Light with a long match at the table and pour over crêpes.

This crêpe batter can be used for all sweet crêpe recipes. Serve with the filling of your choice with whipped cream or ice cream.

For batter, combine crêpe batter ingredients in a food processor.

Cook crêpes till golden brown on both sides. Transfer to a plate and cover.

Add orange and lemon juice to the butter-sugar mixture.

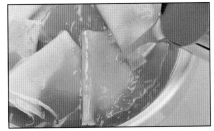

Fold crêpes into quarters and arrange them in ovenproof dish. Pour sauce over.

Chilled Grand Marnier Soufflé

A spectacular dessert.

Preparation time:
    35 minutes
Chilling time:
    Several hours
Cooking time:
    10 minutes
Serves 6

---

8 eggs, separated
1/3 cup sugar
1/3 cup Grand
    Marnier
1 tablespoon finely
    shredded orange peel
1 cup orange juice
1 teaspoon vanilla
2 envelopes
    unflavored gelatin

1/4 cup cold water
2 cups whipping
    cream, whipped
Fresh orange sections
Strips of orange peel
Whipped cream
Sliced almonds,
    toasted

---

1 Cut a piece of foil 2 inches longer than the circumference of a 6-cup soufflé dish. Fold foil in half lengthwise. Wrap foil around the outside edge of the dish, extending 2 inches above the rim. Secure with string or tape. Lightly grease the bottom and sides (including the foil) of the dish.

2 In the top of a double boiler combine egg yolks, sugar, Grand Marnier, orange peel, orange juice, and vanilla. Beat with an electric mixer over simmering water till mixture thickens. In a small bowl or saucepan sprinkle gelatin over cold water. Stand bowl in hot water and stir till gelatin dissolves or cook and stir over low heat till dissolved. Add to egg mixture. Chill, stirring occasionally, till the mixture begins to set (should be the consistency of corn syrup). Remove from the refrigerator (mixture will continue to set).

3 Beat egg whites in a clean dry bowl till stiff peaks form. When gelatin mixture is thicker (should be the consistency of unbeaten egg whites) fold in beaten egg whites. Fold in whipped cream. Spoon into prepared soufflé dish. Refrigerate several hours or till firm.

4 To serve, carefully remove foil collar. Garnish with orange sections, orange peel, whipped cream, and toasted almonds.

HINT
Working with gelatin is not difficult if you follow a few simple rules. First sprinkle the gelatin over cold water in a small saucepan. This will soften it and prevent it from forming lumps. Then cook it over the lowest heat setting available till gelatin dissolves, stirring constantly. Grand Marnier is an orange-flavored liqueur.

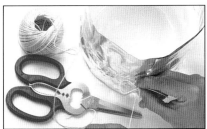

Wrap foil around outside of soufflé dish and secure with string or tape.

Beat egg yolk mixture over barely simmering water till thick.

Sprinkle gelatin over cold water in a small bowl or saucepan to soften.

Spoon mixture into prepared soufflé dish and refrigerate.

61

Fritters with Strawberry Sauce

Preparation time:
30 minutes
Cooking time:
10–15 minutes
Serves 6–8

FRITTERS	SAUCE
1 cup water	*¹/₃ cup sugar*
¹/₂ cup currants or raisins	*¹/₄ cup water*
¹/₄ cup butter or margarine	*8 ounces fresh strawberries*
¹/₄ cup sugar	*2 tablespoons brandy or strawberry liqueur*
1 teaspoon finely shredded orange peel	*Oil for deep-fat frying*
1 cup all-purpose flour	*Powdered sugar*
3 eggs, lightly beaten	

1 For fritters, in a saucepan combine water, currants or raisins, butter or margarine, ¹/₄ cup sugar, and orange peel. Bring to a boil. Gradually stir in flour and beat with a wooden spoon till smooth. Cool slightly. Gradually add eggs, beating well after each addition; set aside.

2 For sauce, in a saucepan cook and stir ¹/₃ cup sugar and water till sugar dissolves. Add strawberries and simmer, uncovered, for 5 minutes. Transfer to a food processor. Cover; process 30 seconds or till smooth. Stir in liqueur.

3 Drop dough by rounded teaspoonfuls into hot oil (375°). Cook 3 to 4 minutes or till golden brown, turning once. Drain on paper towels. Sift powdered sugar over warm fritters. Serve immediately with sauce.

Note: Kiwifruit, mangoes, raspberries, or blueberries can replace the strawberries, if desired.

Stir flour into butter-sugar mixture in saucepan till smooth.

Add strawberries to syrup and simmer, uncovered, for 5 minutes.

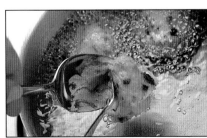

Gently drop dough by rounded
teaspoonfuls into hot oil.

Fritters will puff and turn golden brown
when done. Drain on paper towels.

INDEX

Almonds, Trout with 24
Apple Flan, French 57

Beans with
  Tomatoes 48
Beef
  and Red Wine
    Casserole 28
  Fillet in Pastry Crust
    with Horseradish
    Cream 27

Cassoulet 32
Casserole
  Beef and Red
    Wine 28
  Lamb, with
    Vegetables 38
  Eggplant and
    Tomato 52
Cheese Soufflés with
  Crab Sauce 14
Chicken
  Roast with Grapes 40
  Tarragon Cream 42
  with Peppers 44
Cod Pâté, Chilled, with
  Melba Toast 10
Crêpes Suzette 58

Eggplant and Tomato
  Casserole 52

Fish Fillets with Butter
  Sauce 22
Flan
  Tomato and Olive, 8
  French Apple 57
French Onion Soup 5
Fritters with
  Strawberry Sauce 62

Gougére, Ham and
  Mushroom 12
Grand Marnier Soufflé,
  Chilled 60

Ham and Mushroom
  Gougére 12

Lamb
  Casserole with
    Vegetables 38
Lamb Navarin 38
Leek Tart 18

Melba Toast, Chilled
  Cod Pâté with 10

Omelette, Potato with
  Olive Topping 16

Pâté, Chilled Cod with
  Melba Toast 10
Pepper Steak 30
Pork with Cabbage and
  Plums 34

Potato
  Cake 50
  Puffs 54
  Omelette with Olive
    Topping 16
Prawn Croustade 6

Ratatouille 52
Roast Chicken with
  Grapes 40

Salad, Watercress 47
Sauce
  Crab, Cheese Soufflés
    with 14
  Butter, Fish Fillets
    with 22
  Dijon Mustard, Veal
    with 36
Soup,
  French Onion 5
Soufflé
  Cheese with Crab
    Sauce 14
  Chilled Grand
    Marnier 60
Snapper, Baked with
  Garlic and Tomatoes
  21
Steak, Pepper 30

Tapenade 16
Tarragon Cream
  Chicken 42
Tart, Leek 18
Tomato and Olive
  Flan 8
Trout with Almonds 24

Veal with Dijon
  Mustard Sauce 36

Watercress Salad 47

The Ruins at
Machu
Picchu

by Sharon Gordon

MODERN CURRICULUM PRESS
Pearson Learning Group

Picture a beautiful city set on a mountaintop, miles high in the air. Imagine this city filled with deep green landscape, magnificent waterfalls, and stone buildings that are as breathtaking as the classical structures of Europe. Now imagine this city is over four hundred years old and was home to the mighty Inca people. You have just discovered the ancient city of Machu Picchu in Peru, South America!

The Inca's amazing empire stretched from the Pacific Ocean on the west to the Amazon River Basin on the east. It included land in Colombia in the north, all the way to Chile in the south. Because it was so vast, the Incas called it the "Land of the Four Quarters."

3

For many hundreds of years, the Incas were just one of many native tribes living in this area. But by the 1200s they had moved into the Cuzco Valley. By the early 1500s, they controlled much of the land and had conquered the other native tribes. The Inca Empire lasted for a little over a hundred years. It ended in the 1500s when Spanish explorers began to arrive in South America. The Spanish forced the Incas off the ancient Inca land. Most of the Inca cities were destroyed, and along with them, much of their history and heritage.

That is why the discovery of the ancient ruins of Machu Picchu is so important. In 1911, Hiram Bingham, an archaeologist from the United States, came to Peru to learn about its past. He and others hoped to find and excavate ancient cities of the Incas. They had heard stories about incredible fortress cities hidden high up in the Andes Mountains.

Bingham and a Peruvian soldier began their exciting journey from the city of Cuzco. They started by exploring the area around the Urubamba River. As they traveled, they saw the ruins of many Inca villages. They also saw the ruins of temples and other stone buildings as they followed the river.

They passed an Inca quarry, where huge stones were cut and carved from the mountainside. These stones were used to make buildings throughout the empire. Bingham was amazed that the Incas were able to make such sturdy structures with no modern tools.

After a few days of travel, Bingham and his friend came upon a tiny village. They met a farmer who lived in a hut. He told them about some ruins he had seen and offered to show them the way.

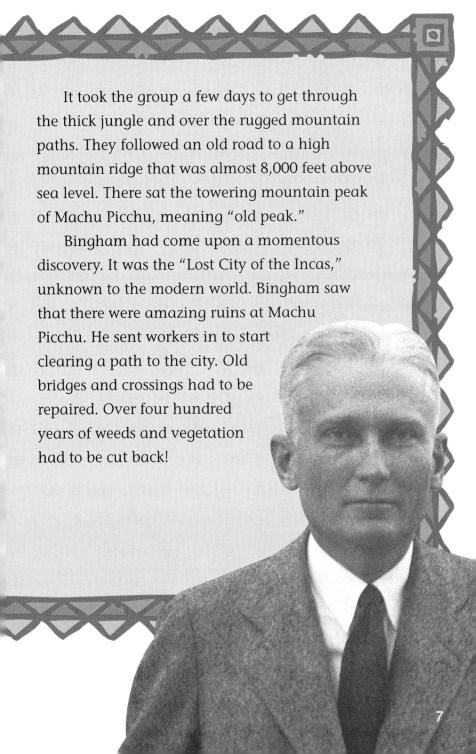

It took the group a few days to get through the thick jungle and over the rugged mountain paths. They followed an old road to a high mountain ridge that was almost 8,000 feet above sea level. There sat the towering mountain peak of Machu Picchu, meaning "old peak."

Bingham had come upon a momentous discovery. It was the "Lost City of the Incas," unknown to the modern world. Bingham saw that there were amazing ruins at Machu Picchu. He sent workers in to start clearing a path to the city. Old bridges and crossings had to be repaired. Over four hundred years of weeds and vegetation had to be cut back!

During this time, Bingham went back to the United States to plan for a return trip to Machu Picchu. A year later, he and a team of archaeologists arrived at the site to study the ruins. They had to spend months digging out the brush and growth that covered the city and its buildings. They were especially careful to excavate tree roots that had grown in between the layers of stone of the structures.

Bingham knew right away that Machu Picchu was a fortress city. The Indians used it as a secret hideaway. Some think it might have been built to hide from the Spanish explorers. Or, it might have been constructed by the early Inca tribes to protect them from other enemies.

The reason Machu Picchu remained a secret for so long was that it was so hard to reach. Sitting on a mountaintop, it had steep slopes on all sides—too steep to climb. Only one side of the mountain could be used to make a path or road to the top. And the Incas made sure this single approach was carefully guarded! Here, the city was protected by colossal double walls—sixteen feet high and three feet thick. A dry moat was built in between the walls and around the city for extra protection. And, if that weren't enough, a giant gate made it enemy-proof!

A watchtower stood on the inside of the city gate. It was built on a giant stone slab. It had eight inner rooms with two windows that gave the Incas a good view of the valley below. From there, guards could see any enemy who approached the mountain city.

Because Machu Picchu was built into the side of a mountain, the city was made up of many different levels, or terraces. In between each of the terraces were stone stairways. Bingham and his team found over a hundred different stairways at Machu Picchu. Sometimes, several flights of stairs were carved out of one block of granite!

The leveled terraces got higher and higher until they reached the top of the city. The Incas grew crops and raised animals on the terraces. The terraces also helped save the city from erosion by wind and rain.

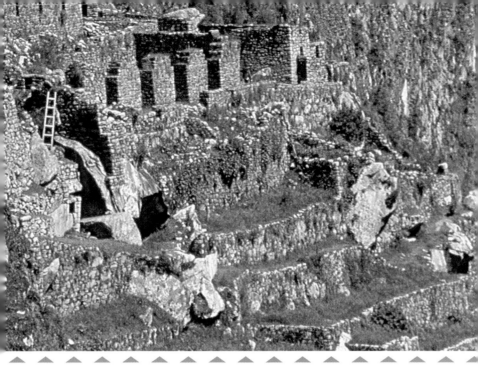

How did the Incas get all those large stones up the mountain? No one is certain. But it wasn't easy! Of course, some stones were found on the mountain. But others had to be brought up from distant quarries. Often, they had to be carried over the river and up steep paths.

Once the stones were brought to the proper place, they were cut and shaped by Inca stonecutters. These experts then used stone hammers and wet sand to polish the finished rock. The stones were moved into place by strong ropes and human strength. It's difficult to imagine the amount of time and effort it took to make a single dwelling.

Altogether, 143 stone buildings were found at Machu Picchu. About eighty of them were houses similar to those in other Inca cities. They were made of stone and had thatched roofs. Often, a group of homes surrounded an area where animals, such as llamas or goats, could graze. Other dwellings were located around areas where crops, such as corn or potatoes, could grow.

The remaining structures of Machu Picchu were palaces, temples, and places for special ceremonies. The Incas considered this mountain city to be sacred. At the very top of Machu Picchu was an area called the sacred plaza. It contained three separate temples: the great temple, the main temple, and a special house for the Inca priests.

The Incas believed in many gods, but the sun was the most important. They hoped this god would bring good weather and abundant crops. A special stone terrace with a tall clock-like top was found near the temple ruins. Many people believe it might have been a sundial. It probably helped the Incas keep track of the seasons, so that on June 21 they could celebrate the Festival of the Sun God.

Inside the main temple of Machu Picchu were three large windows in a unique shape. This shape, called a trapezoid, had four sides that became thinner at the top. Nearly all Inca buildings had this design, and it could be found in their doors and openings too.

Where did the Incas find fresh, flowing water to use up in their mountain homes? Hundreds of years before faucets and bottled water were invented, the Incas thought of a clever plan to bring water to their city. They built a one-and-a-half-mile-long channel from the springs of a nearby peak into Machu Picchu. The channel crossed the moat that surrounded the city, ran under the city walls, and into what was called the "Stairway of Fountains." This was a series of stone basins which were connected by stairs. The spring water flowed from the top basin down through the different levels of the city. The Incas could bring their water jars to the basins to fill for drinking, cooking, cleaning, or bathing.

What is also amazing about Inca buildings is that the stones of their buildings were put in place without any mortar, or cement, to hold them together. Over all these years, the stone buildings have stood through all kinds of weather. In fact, the lack of mortar may have been a good thing. It may have protected their buildings from earthquakes, which occur quite often in the Andes Mountains. Because there was no cement holding them together, the stones were able to shift as the Earth shook.

Machu Picchu, like many other Inca cities, was carefully planned. There were special ways to care for all the citizens of the empire. There were structures for homes, for storing food, and even for storing fresh water. We must look with respect at the skilled workers who designed and built this mountain paradise one stone at a time.

Much of Machu Picchu has been restored and repaired. It is a wonderful place to see. Many of the old thatched-roof homes were rebuilt. Today these buildings give visitors a real sense of what it would have been like to live in this remote mountaintop city among the mighty Incas.